LEGO NINJAGO
Masters of Spinjitzu

TOURNAMENT OF ELEMENTS

Story and art by Blue Ocean
Additional art by Caravan Studio

"Lost Scrolls of Spinjitzu"
written by Greg Farshtey

Ⓛ Ⓑ

LITTLE, BROWN BOOKS FOR YOUNG READERS
www.lbkids.co.uk

LITTLE, BROWN BOOKS FOR YOUNG READERS

First published in the US in 2015 by Little, Brown and Company
First published in the UK in 2015 by Hodder & Stoughton

1 3 5 7 9 10 8 6 4 2

LEGO, the LEGO logo, the Brick and Knob configurations, the Minifigure
and NINJAGO are trademarks of the LEGO Group.

Produced by Hodder & Stoughton under licence from the LEGO Group.
© 2015 The LEGO Group

Comic artwork © 2015 by Blue Ocean Entertainment AG, Germany

A CIP catalogue record for this book
is available from the British Library.

ISBN 978-1-51020-049-4

Printed and bound in the United States of America

Little, Brown Books for Young Readers
An imprint of
Hachette Children's Group
Part of Hodder & Stoughton
Carmelite House
50 Victoria Embankment
London EC4Y 0DZ

An Hachette UK Company
www.hachette.co.uk

KAI

Kai is something of a hothead, which is fitting, since he commands the element of Fire. He is the son of a blacksmith and the brother of Nya.

COLE

Cole is a very calm and intelligent member of the ninja. He commands the element of Earth, giving him great physical strength and durability.

JAY

Always telling jokes, Jay is the most lighthearted of the ninja. He can harness the elements of Lightning and Wind to create a Spinjitzu tornado of pure electricity.

LLOYD

Lloyd loves his father, Garmadon. Once, this almost drove him to evil, but his inherently good nature instead led him to join the ninja and command the element of Energy.

SENSEI GARMADON

As a young boy, he was infected with evil. But eventually, his brother, Sensei Wu, would save him. He is Lloyd's father, and he currently controls the element of Creation.

NYA

Although she is not a ninja, Nya is very capable of defending herself. She is Kai's younger sister and a key ally

ZANE

Zane is the most reserved and serious of the ninja, but he is also the most respectful. His affinity for Ice allows him to freeze objects and perform a chilly Spinjitzu attack.

SKYLOR

Skylor is the daughter of the nefarious Master Chen and is the current Elemental Master of Amber, which allows her

TOURNAMENT OF ELEMENTS

What came before...

The ninja were involved in an epic battle with the Golden Master. When everything else failed, Zane sacrificed himself to defeat the Overlord. After the battle, Zane was honored with a titanium statue in the center of Ninjago City. Devastated by the loss of their friend, Kai, Cole, Jay, and Lloyd disbanded the ninja team.

But soon after, the team discovered there was a possibility that Zane was still alive. In order to find out for sure, the ninja must travel to a mysterious island and enter the dangerous Tournament of Elements, arranged by Master Chen. But is Master Chen all that he seems, or is he connected to the most feared warriors in the history of ninja: the Anacondrai?!

CHAPTER 1

REMEMBER, MY NINJA, WE ARE STRANGERS IN A STRANGE LAND. MASTER CHEN HAS INVITED US HERE IN KINDNESS, BUT I DO NOT TRUST HIM.

DO NOT BE DECEIVED BY CHEN'S GENEROSITY— YOU WILL PAY DEARLY FOR EVERY BITE.

MUT YOU MUFFT FFAY ONE FFING FOR HIM: VE CAKE IFF DELIFFIOUFF! MUNFF!

YOU SHOULDN'T SPEAK WITH YOUR MOUTH FULL.

SENSEI GARMADON, IT WOULD PLEASE ME TO WELCOME YOU IN MY CHAMBERS. CLOUSE WILL BE THERE IN A MOMENT TO COLLECT YOU AND ACCOMPANY YOU HERE. CHEN, OVER AND OUT!

DON'T ACCEPT THE INVITATION. IT'S TOO DANGEROUS.

THAT WAS NO INVITATION. I HAVE NO CHOICE.

JUFFT FFEE IF HE DAREFF TO COME AND GET YOU!

DO NOT WORRY, MY FRIENDS, I CAN TAKE GOOD CARE OF MYSELF.

KNOCK KNOCK

I'M COMING.

HE'LL PROBABLY BE BACK SOON.

I WOULDN'T BE SO SURE OF THAT.

COLE, COULD YOU STOP EATING FOR ONE MOMENT!?

I MUFFT BUILD UP MY FTRENGFF IN CAFE I HAVE TO FIGHT FOON!

I WOULD LIKE TO EMPHASIZE ONCE AGAIN HOW PLEASED I AM BY YOUR VISIT. MY HOSPITALITY IS GREAT AND YOU SHALL AT LAST HAVE YOUR OWN CLOSED ROOM...

KLICK

WOOSH

WELL, MY FRIEND, HOW DO YOU LIKE YOUR NEW ROOM? OR SHOULD I SAY CAGE?!

NO MATTER WHAT YOU ARE PLANNING TO DO, YOU WILL NEVER SUCCEED IN DIVIDING THE NINJA!

WE SHALL SEE.

CHAPTER 2

SHHHHRRRRRRKKKKKK

UGH!

CRASH

WHEW!

NOT FIGHT FAIR! COWARD, YOU COME BACK!

SORRY, KARLOF, BUT I'VE GOTTA RUN. ENJOY PLAYING WITH YOUR BIG MARBLE.

COME ON, KAI, LET'S GET OUT OF THIS TUNNEL AT LAST!

OH GREAT, HOW ARE WE SUPPOSED TO GET OUT NOW? I CAN'T STAND SPIDERS!

WE MUST HELP SKYLOR!

WHY SHOULD WE HELP HER? SHE'S OUR SURPRISE OPPONENT—OR HAVE YOU ALREADY FORGOTTEN?

CHAPTER 3

SENSEI WU ONCE TOLD ME ABOUT PLANTS THAT GIVE YOU VAGUE VISIONS OF THE FUTURE.

LET'S HOPE IT WAS ONE OF THOSE!

I HOPE HE'S GOING TO WAKE UP SOON.

HE'S WAKING UP!

WHERE IS NYA?! THE ANACONDRAI! UM, WHAT HAPPENED?

NYA? ANACONDRAI? ARE YOU OKAY? THE PLANT SENT YOU OFF TO DREAMLAND FOR AN HOUR!

THAT WAS MORE THAN JUST A DREAM...IT WAS A WARNING! MY FATHER WAS RIGHT FROM THE START. WE CAN'T TRUST MASTER CHEN. WE NEED TO DEFEAT HIM!

CHAPTER 5

WHICH WAY NOW?

WE'VE BEEN ON THE MOVE FOR AGES NOW AND STILL HAVE NO CLUE AS TO WHERE MASTER CHEN IS HOLDING MY FATHER PRISONER.

CHEN IS SURE TO SET A NEW TRAP FOR US.

WE HAVE NO OTHER CHOICE BUT TO TRUST OUR INSTINCTS. AND MINE TELLS ME: THAT WAY.

LITTLE DO THE NINJA KNOW THAT MASTER CHEN HAS SENT GRIFFIN TURNER AFTER THEM.

CHAPTER 6

THERE IS NO SIGN OF COLE.

THE SMALL FANGFISHES ATTACK THE NINJA, BUT THEY ARE TOO SMALL TO FRIGHTEN THE HEROES.

BLUBBER BLUBBLUBB BLUBB BLUBB.

BLUBB BLUBB BLUBB?!?

LLOYD GIVES THE SIGN TO RESURFACE. THEY NEED A PLAN...AND MORE AIR.

WHAT NEW TRICK IS THIS, NOW?

IF THE VORTEX GETS ANY FASTER IT WILL PULL US DOWN!

SWOOSH!

I THINK... THAT IS COLE!

NNG!

UNDERWATER, THE GIANT FANGFISH FINDS OUT WHAT SPINJITZU IS!

I HOPE YOUR SUSPICION IS RIGHT!

IT HAS TO BE... UNLESS IT'S ANOTHER TRAP?!

BLUBB BLUBB COLE!

BLUBB BLUBB BLUBB CAVE BLUBB BLUBB!

BLUBB BLUBB BLUBB THIS WAY BLUBB BLUBB!

SNAP!

SNAP!

CHAPTER 7

NINJA, YOU HAVE DONE WELL IN PASSING MASTER CHEN'S TESTS. I AM PROUD OF YOU. WE HAVE PREPARED A FEAST FOR YOU BELOW. PLEASE, ENJOY.

FATHER! YOU'RE OKAY?!

SENSEI GARMADON IS FINE! TIME TO EAT!!

I'M SOOO HUNGRY!

GUYS, DO YOU THINK THIS IS SOME KIND OF TRICK?

I HOPE NOT. I'M STARVING. I COULD USE AN HOUR TO JUST SIT AND RELAX.

THESE NOODLES ARE DELICIOUS! EAT UP.

I CAN HARDLY SEE THE NOODLES IN FRONT OF MY FACE!

SLURPPP knurpss knurpss

WHAT'S WITH ALL THIS SMOKE? SOMETHING'S NOT RIGHT HERE.

JAY WAS RIGHT. THIS IS ANOTHER TRAP.

OOAAH!
HYAAAA! TAKE THIS.
AARGH!
POW!
...AND THAT!
KRACH!!!
BOOMMM
YOU REALLY THINK A LITTLE BIT OF SMOKE AND A FEW RODENTS CAN STOP US?
WUUUSSHHH!!!
FEEEEEP!!
WATCH THIS! WE'LL SPIN YOUR SMOKE AWAY.
YOU'RE HELPLESS WITHOUT YOUR LITTLE RATS AND A BIT OF SMOKE, AREN'T YOU!?
SEARCHING FOR A WAY OUT, AREN'T YOU?
NINJA...

EVERYONE OKAY?

ALIVE—BUT JUST BARELY.

WE HAVE TO FIND ZANE!

THEY'RE DISTRACTED... THAT'S MY CHANCE!

BYE-BYE!

SWIT!

LOOKS LIKE ZANE FOUND US.

ZANE!

TELL US EVERYTHING, ZANE!

YES, WHERE YOU'VE BEEN AND...

...!

WE THOUGHT YOU WERE...

WELL DONE, NINJA! SENSEI WU AND SENSEI GARMADON HAVE TAUGHT YOU WELL.

FOR NOW, YOUR SENSEI MAY REJOIN YOU, AND YOU HAVE THE NIGHT TO RELAX AND REST BEFORE YOUR **REAL** TRIALS BEGIN.

LATER.

I'M GLAD YOU'RE ALL RIGHT, FATHER. BUT WE HAVE SO MANY QUESTIONS...

LIKE, WHEN ARE WE GOING TO EAT?

NO, KNUCKLEHEAD.

THAT SHAPE-SHIFTER—SHE KNEW WHAT ZANE LOOKED LIKE. BUT THE ONLY WAY SHE COULD HAVE KNOWN...

...IS IF SHE'D SEEN HIM.

DOES THAT MEAN ZANE IS ALIVE?! AND HERE?!

THE LOST SCROLLS OF SPINJITZU

By Greg Farshtey

Welcome to the Ninjago World

Ninjago Island was created long ago by the First Spinjitzu Master, using the power of the Golden Weapons. Although the Ninjago world was initially a place of peace and light, evil arose in the form of the Overlord, who wished dominion over the planet. With no end to the struggle in sight, the First Spinjitzu Master took the drastic step of splitting Ninjago Island in half. The Overlord and his followers were trapped on a portion that came to be known as the Island of Darkness.

This was not the end of threats to the world. The first Serpentine War pitted humans against snake warriors. One of the First Spinjitzu Master's sons, Garmadon, was corrupted by darkness and tried to conquer the world, only to be defeated by his brother, Wu. Sensei Wu would go on to defend the planet against various menaces for years to come, before eventually recruiting a team of young ninja to help him.

Ninjago is a geographically diverse land, with volcanoes, deserts, ice caps, dense forests and jungles, toxic bogs, and more. Only one city is known to exist—New Ninjago City—but there are long-lost cities dotting the landscape. There are also a large number of villages and farming communities.

The ninja's adventures have carried them all over the land, and they have saved Ninjago Island many times over. Time will tell what excitement the future has in store for them!

Ninjago map

1. Four Weapons Blacksmith
2. Wu's Monastery
3. Caves of Despair
4. Frozen Wasteland & Wailing Alps (Hybnobrai Serpentine Tomb)
5. Floating Ruins
6. Forest of Tranquility
7. Fire Temple (Fangblade location and passageway to the Underworld)
8. Jamanaki Village
9. Forest & Lloyd's Tree House
10. Destiny's Bounty
11. Ed and Edna's Junkyard
12. Cemetery of Souls (Fangpyre Serpentine tomb)
13. Darkley's School for Bad Boys/Sensei Wu's Academy
14. Mountain of a Million Steps (Constrictai Serpentine tomb and Serpentine main hive)
15. Toxic Bogs (Venomari tomb)
16. Ninjago City
17. The (Formerly) Lost City of Oroborous
18. Mega Monster Amusement Park (Fangblade location)
19. BirchWood Forest
20. Mistake's Tea Shop (in a small village)
21. Serpentine Pyramid (Fangblade location)
22. Cole's Hometown (Fangblade location)
23. Torch Fire Mountain
24. Scattered Canyon
25. Golden Peaks (Birthplace of the Golden Weapons of Spinjitzu)
26. Sea of Sand
27. Crash Course Canyon
28. Glacier Barrens
29. Badlands
30. Lighthouse
31. Master Chen's Island
32. Garmadon's Sanctuary
33. Samurai X cave
34. Power Substation Lightning Farm
35. Hiroshi's Labyrinth
36. Kryptarium Prison
37. Corridor of Elders

30

LOCATIONS

Mr. Chen's Noodle Houses

Mr. Chen's Noodle Houses, renowned for their many and varied types of noodle dishes, are the most popular restaurants in the Ninjago world. The diners might not enjoy themselves quite so much if they knew that Mr. Chen is actually Master Chen, an evil genius planning to conquer the world, and that the noodles

were made by slave laborers. Then again, diners might...those noodles are awfully good.

Underground Noodle Factory

Once elemental fighters lose a match (and their powers), they find themselves trapped in Master Chen's noodle factory. This work camp is heavily guarded by Chen's henchmen. Using giant machinery, laborers work hard to make the noodles. No one had ever escaped from the noodle factory until Cole and Zane led a mass breakout of the workers.

The Corridor of Elders

The Corridor of Elders is a passage in Echo Canyon, the natural landmark that divides Ninjago Island. It is the  quickest route through the canyon and is renowned for the engravings of historical figures etched into its walls. It is the site of the final battle between the ninja and Chen's Anacondrai warriors.

Chen's Fortress

Concealed by Clouse's magic spells, Chen's secret island is home to his fortress and private army. It is considered to be impenetrable and is loaded with trapdoors, booby traps, hidden passages, and other dangers. Catacombs far beneath lead both to Chen's underground noodle work camp and the Anacondrai temple.

Anacondrai Temple

Deep inside Chen's island are the ruins of an ancient Anacondrai temple. This is where Master Chen carries out his dark ceremonies, using his staff to rob the elemental  fighters of their powers. Often, it is the last place the fighters see before they are consigned to labor in the noodle factory forever. It is also home to Clouse's pet Anacondrai snake.

HEROES

Kai

Kai and his sister, Nya, got used to taking care of themselves from an early age, so Kai still prefers to do things on his own. At first, working on a team was a challenge for him. Despite his hot temper, he has grown to become the dedicated young Ninja of Fire and the leader of the team.

Acting first and asking questions later has always been Kai's style. And for him, the lure of this tournament is the chance to prove he is better than all the other fighters. But nothing is more important than his friends. So when push comes to shove, Kai steps up to do the right thing— even when Skylor tries to distract him.

Element: Fire
Color: Red
Home Base: Destiny's Bounty
Weapon: Sword
Hobbies: Blacksmithing and cooking

Jay

Jay is a fast-talking, fun-loving, and inventive Ninja of Lightning. His favorite thing about being a ninja is the adventure...well, that and being around Nya, on whom he has a big crush. Jay is best known for his inventions, some of which work, some of which fail spectacularly. More than once, his gadgets have saved the day.

As the ninja head for the tournament, there is a lot of tension between Jay and Cole due to their mutual interest in Nya. Competing in the tournament only makes things worse, but eventually they realize that what they—and the team as a whole—are fighting for is more important than their personal quarrels.

Element: Lightning
Color: Blue
Home Base: Destiny's Bounty
Weapon: Nunchakus
Hobbies: Inventing and tinkering

Cole

The Ninja of Earth takes the team's missions very seriously and spends a lot of time planning strategy and tactics. For that reason, he finds the dispute with Jay over Nya to be an annoying distraction at a dangerous time.

Cole has always done his best to come across as serious-minded and fearless. But it didn't take long for his friends to discover that there were things Cole was afraid of, such as dragons. Cole learned to overcome that fear and is hopeful that means he can do the same if he ever again encounters something frightening.

Element: Earth	
Color: Black	
Home Base: Destiny's Bounty	
Weapon: Scythe	
Hobbies: Rock climbing; dancing	

Zane

Zane is a robot called a Nindroid and the Ninja of Ice. He is extremely intelligent but often struggles with things like humor. Despite this, he values his friendships with the other ninja and his relationship with an artificial intelligence named Pixal.

Zane apparently gave his life to defeat the Overlord in an earlier adventure and was believed gone forever. In truth, he was being held captive by Master Chen. By overcoming his own fears and insecurities, Zane emerges stronger than ever before as the Titanium Ninja. Reuniting with his team, he is ready to play an important role in the battles to come.

Element: Ice	
Color: White	
Home Base: Destiny's Bounty	
Weapon: Shurikens	
Hobbies: Working with Pixal	

Lloyd

Lloyd is the son of Sensei Garmadon. When the ninja first met him, he was trying hard to be a villain like his father. But he eventually discovered that it is more rewarding fighting beside the ninja than against them. To Lloyd's surprise, he turned out to be the legendary Green Ninja. For a brief time, he ascended to even greater power as the Golden Ninja, but he gave those powers up for the benefit of his friends.

His age advanced by magic, Lloyd has now become one of the leaders of the team. It is his drive and his belief that Zane is still alive somewhere that keeps the ninja squad from falling apart. He succeeds in reuniting his teammates and taking on the challenge of the tournament, even though he knows that every fighter wants the chance to take down the Green Ninja.

Element: Energy
Color: Green
Home Base: Destiny's Bounty
Weapon: Katana
Hobbies: Training; trying to build a relationship with his father

Nya

For too long, Nya has been known as "Kai's sister" or "Jay's girlfriend." She has longed to carve out an identity for herself and be a valuable part of the team. To accomplish this, she secretly built the Samurai X armor and went into action without any of the ninja being any the wiser—at least not until Kai found out.

Nya is both inventive and resourceful. When the ninja disappear on Chen's island, Nya is the one who is able to track down where they are. She even manages to infiltrate Chen's operation for a brief time. Nya hopes that she has proven herself to be considered for ninja training.

Element: None...yet!
Color: Red
Home Base: Destiny's Bounty
Weapon: : Golden Nick Daggers; Samurai X armor
Hobbies: Mechanics

Sensei Wu

One of the two sons of the First Spinjitzu Master, Wu is ancient and very wise. He fought alone for centuries against many terrible villains in order to defend Ninjago. But he eventually realized that he could not continue to do the job alone. He recruited four young men and trained them to be ninja. With his guidance, they not only learned the fighting skills they needed, they also learned how to be heroes.

As time has passed, Sensei Wu has begun to contemplate retirement. He believes that he can leave the fate of Ninjago safely in the hands of his students. But before he can do so, he has to aid them one more time to defeat a villain as evil as any he has ever faced.

Element: Creation

Color: White

Home Base: Destiny's Bounty

Weapon: Nin-jo

Hobbies: Drinking tea

Sensei Garmadon

The brother of Sensei Wu, Garmadon was corrupted in his youth and became consumed by evil. He was banished to the Underworld for thousands of years by Wu, but he returned in recent times to battle his brother and the ninja team repeatedly. Finally cured of the darkness inside him, Garmadon took a vow of peace and took over the training of the team. He also worked to rebuild his relationship with his son, Lloyd, although so much time apart made it difficult.

During the battle with the Anacondrai warriors, the spirits of the original Anacondrai had to be freed from the Cursed Realm if the ninja had any hope of winning. Garmadon realized that, in order for this to happen, someone would have to take their place in that otherworldly realm. He made the sacrifice to save his world and his friends. A statue of him now graces the Corridor of Elders.

Element: Creation

Color: Black

Home Base: Destiny's Bounty

Weapon: Nin-Jo

Hobbies: Meditation; trying to build a relationship with Lloyd

VILLAINS

Master Chen

Mr. Chen is best known throughout the Ninjago world as the owner of a chain of successful noodle houses. What few realize is that Mr. Chen is in reality Master Chen, an evil mastermind with plans to start a second Serpentine War.

Ages ago, Chen was a respected sensei with a "win at all costs" philosophy. His double-dealing led to a war between humans and the Serpentine, which eventually resulted in Chen being exiled to a remote island. There he began to build a criminal empire, using his noodle houses as a front for illegal activities.

Chen's ultimate plan is to transform his followers into Anacondrai warriors and conquer the Ninjago world. To do this, he needs samples of every elemental power. He stages a Tournament of Elements at his island fortress to lure warriors there, only to steal their elemental abilities from them. With those energies, he turns his minions into true Anacondrai serpents.

Leading his army of warriors off the island, Chen succeeds in conquering a large portion of Ninjago, despite opposition by the ninja. He is finally defeated when the heroes succeed in releasing the spirits of honorable Anacondrai from the Cursed Realm. These spirits, angered by Chen's actions, banish him and his followers to the Cursed Realm forever.

Personality: Chen loves to manipulate others and turns his enemies against each other in order to weaken them. He is ruthless, cunning, and shows no mercy to those who oppose him.

Weapon: Staff of Elements

Hobbies: World conquest

Clouse

Clouse is a powerful sorcerer and Master Chen's second in command. He uses dark magic to keep the ninja from winning in the Tournament of Elements is completely devoted to the service of his master.

In his youth, Clouse was a student of Chen's, as was Garmadon. Clouse lost out on the chance to be favored by Chen when Garmadon cheated him out of a victory. Clouse has harbored a hatred of Garmadon ever since.

Clouse has been exiled to the Cursed Realm by Garmadon.

Personality: Clouse is bitter, vengeful, and power-hungry. He sees his service to Chen as the best way to achieve what he has always dreamed of.

Weapon: None, but he is an adept spell caster

Hobbies: Studying magic

The Other Anacondrai

Chen's gang of criminals is transformed into Anacondrai warriors as part of the villain's plan to conquer Ninjago. Some of his henchmen include:

Zugu

A former sumo wrestler, later a general in Chen's army. This armored warrior is particularly skilled with a crossbow.

Eyezor

Chen's other general, the one-eyed Eyezor doesn't talk much, but he and his Anacondrai sword are plenty intimidating.

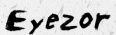

Kapau and Chop

These two best friends don't have much in terms of skill or talent, but they are determined to move up in Chen's army. Kapau and Chope use Anacondrai blades as weapons.

Pythor

In a strange twist of fate, the battle against Chen forced the ninja to ally with one of their worst enemies, Pythor. The last survivor of the Anacondrai tribe, Pythor first met the ninja when he was trying to unite the other Serpentine tribes and unleash the horrible Great Devourer on Ninjago. Later, he allied with the Overlord in yet another plot to conquer the world and destroy the ninja.

This time, though, the hunter is the hunted. Chen needs Pythor to complete his spell to turn his followers into Anacondrai, so Pythor needs the ninja's help to survive. In the end, it is Pythor who discovers that, by releasing the spirits of his deceased tribemates from the Cursed Realm, Chen's false Anacondrai can be defeated. Pythor survives the final battle with Chen, but where he may be now is unknown.

Element: None
Color: Purple and white
Home Base: None
Weapon: Sword
Hobbies: Lying; plotting;
betrayal; survival

THE ELEMENTAL FIGHTERS

Master Chen's tournament draws elemental warriors from all over the world to his island. They are all descendants of the Elemental Masters, powerful beings who served as guardians of the First Spinjitzu Master long ago. All of them are stripped of their powers during the tournament by Master Chen with one possible exception: Skylor was turned back into human form, but it is unknown if she still has her powers.

Ash—Master of Smoke

Ash can transform himself into a cloud of smoke at will, appearing and disappearing all over and making it almost impossible to lay a finger on him. His only known defeat was at the hands of Kai.

Skylor— Master of Absorbtion

The daughter of Master Chen, Skylor is able to absorb other elemental fighters' powers. She eventually turns against her father and becomes an ally of the ninja.

Karlof—Master of Metal

Karlof has the power to turn his body into metal and throw powerhouse punches. He is the first fighter to lose in the tournament when he fails to capture one of the Jade Blades needed to qualify for matches.

Griffin Turner—Master of Speed

Super fast, Griffin is one of the more famous elemental fighters and also something of a show-off. He's one of the first to ally with the ninja.

Jacob Pevsner—Master of Sound

Although Jacob is blind, he can use his sound power to "see" the body heat of those around him. He loses to Skylor in the tournament.

Mr. Pale—Master of Light

Mr. Pale can bend light around his body, making himself invisible. Already shy and quiet, most people don't notice him even when he can be seen.

Shade—Master of Shadows

Shade has the power to travel unseen in the shadows. Very much a loner, Shade trusts no one. At one point, he is falsely accused of being a spy for Master Chen.

Tox—Master of Poison

Able to channel various venoms through her system, Tox is definitely a fighter you won't ever forget. She loses in the tournament to Shade.

Bolobo—Master of Nature

Bolobo is a good-natured sort and one of the older fighters in the tournament. His favored weapon is a staff.

Neuro—Master of Mind

Neuro has telepathic powers, allowing him to anticipate an opponent's next move. He can also use his abilities to give his foes headaches.

Gravis—Master of Gravity

Able to control one of the fundamental forces of the universe, Gravis can make objects lighter or heavier, walk on walls and ceilings, and more.

Camille—Master of Form

Camille is a shape-shifter. She was defeated by Lloyd Garmadon in a Thunderblades skating match.

POWERFUL OBJECTS

Jade Blades

The jade blades are the prizes in the Tournament of Elements. Anyone who wins a match gets a blade. Although they are a bit unwieldy, they are quite useful as weapons. The jade blades are carved from the bones of Anacondrai warriors, giving them great symbolic significance to Master Chen.

The Book of Spells

Clouse's most prized possession, The Book of Spells, is a volume of dark magic. The sorcerer uses the spells inscribed on its pages to empower himself and strike at the ninja. The most powerful spell in the book is the Spell of Transformation, which will enable Chen and his followers to turn themselves into Anacondrai warriors.

The Staff of Elements

Master Chen's chosen weapon was forged in the Crystal Caves on his island. It has the ability to absorb the elemental powers of each fallen fighter and then unleash them again. It is instrumental in the

transformation of Chen and his followers, since a sample of every known elemental power is needed to make the spell work.

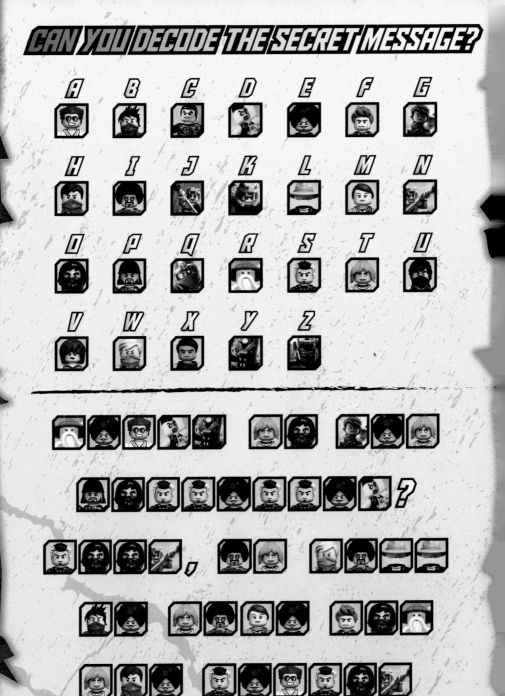